Napa and Sonoma

Travel Guide

Discover the Treasures of California's
Breathtaking Wine Country!

Olivia Reynord

Disclaimer for Pictures:

The photographs and images used in this travel guide are for entertainment only and not depiction of actual location. Every effort have been made to ensure the images are not copyrighted and the author or publisher shall not be liable for any infringement.

CHAPTER 1

INTRODUCTION

About Napa and Sonoma

Nestled in the heart of California's wine country, Napa and Sonoma are two of the most enchanting and celebrated regions for wine enthusiasts and travelers alike. Situated just north of San Francisco, these neighboring valleys boast picturesque landscapes, sprawling vineyards, and charming towns that make for an idyllic escape from the hustle and bustle of city life. The combination of perfect weather, fertile soil, and a long-standing tradition of winemaking has earned Napa and Sonoma an esteemed reputation as premier wine destinations worldwide.

Why Visit Napa and Sonoma

A journey to Napa and Sonoma is not just a wine-tasting escapade but an unforgettable experience that caters to diverse interests and passions. Whether you are a wine connoisseur, an adventure seeker, a history buff, or an avid foodie, these regions have something to offer to everyone. The rolling hills and vineyards create a breathtaking backdrop for exploration and relaxation, while the rich history and culture of the area add depth and character to every visit.

For wine enthusiasts, Napa Valley and Sonoma County offer a staggering array of wineries, ranging from boutique family-owned estates to world-renowned labels. The wine tasting experiences are second to none, where you can savor exquisite vintages while learning about the art of winemaking directly from the passionate vintners themselves.

Nature lovers will find solace in the region's stunning landscapes and outdoor activities. From hot air balloon rides over the vineyards at sunrise to hiking through the scenic trails of the Bothe-Napa Valley State Park, there are numerous opportunities to immerse oneself in nature's beauty.

Those seeking cultural enrichment will be delighted by the region's captivating history and architecture. The area's past is deeply intertwined with the California Gold Rush, and traces of this era can still be found in the historic buildings and landmarks scattered throughout the valleys. Additionally, art galleries, museums, and local events celebrate the creativity and artistic spirit of the community.

For food enthusiasts, the culinary scene is equally impressive. Napa and Sonoma's farm-to-table philosophy means you can indulge in fresh, locally sourced cuisine that beautifully complements the wines of the region. The Michelin-starred restaurants, cozy cafes, and vibrant farmers' markets offer a diverse range of culinary experiences.

Getting to Napa and Sonoma

Reaching Napa and Sonoma is a seamless journey, with various transportation options available. For those arriving by air, the most convenient airport is San Francisco International Airport (SFO). From SFO, you can choose to rent a car or take advantage of shuttle services that operate regularly between the airport and the wine regions.

If you prefer to explore the scenic route, driving to Napa and Sonoma is a delightful option. The valleys are easily accessible from major cities in California, and the drive itself offers breathtaking vistas of vineyards, rolling hills, and meandering rivers.

For a more leisurely and eco-friendly journey, consider traveling by train. Amtrak's Capitol Corridor and San Joaquins routes connect various cities to Napa and Sonoma, allowing you to relax and take in the picturesque scenery along the way.

Once in Napa and Sonoma, getting around is made easy with various transportation options, including rental cars, tour buses, and cycling.

The region's well-maintained roads and bike-friendly trails make exploring the area a pleasurable and immersive experience.

As you embark on your adventure to Napa and Sonoma, prepare to be enchanted by the natural beauty, the delectable wines, and the warm hospitality of the locals. This travel guide will be your trusted companion, revealing the best attractions, activities, dining spots, and travel tips that will help you create cherished memories in these extraordinary valleys. So, pack your bags and get ready to savor the essence of Napa and Sonoma in a journey of a lifetime. Cheers to the beginning of an unforgettable exploration!

CHAPTER 2

ESSENTIAL TRAVEL INFORMATION

Nestled in the heart of California's wine country, Napa and Sonoma offer an enchanting blend of picturesque landscapes, world-class wineries, and cultural experiences. Before embarking on your journey to these charming regions, it is essential to equip yourself with the necessary travel information to make the most of your trip.

Best Time to Visit

The weather in Napa and Sonoma is Mediterranean, making it a year-round destination. However, the best time to visit depends on your preferences and the experiences you seek. Spring (March to May) brings blooming vineyards and milder temperatures, making it ideal for leisurely wine tasting and outdoor activities. Fall (September to November) is equally enchanting, with the grape harvest season in full swing and vibrant foliage setting the landscape aglow. This period is often considered the prime time for wine enthusiasts, offering an opportunity to witness the winemaking process in action.

Summer (June to August) welcomes more tourists due to school vacations, and temperatures can soar.

While this is a popular time for visitors to enjoy the region's beauty, it can be crowded and hot, so plan accordingly. Winter (December to February) is the off-season, offering quieter surroundings and potentially lower prices. Although some wineries may close or have limited hours, the region's beauty never fades, and you can still indulge in wine tastings, cozy up by the fireplace, and savor the charm of the season.

Weather and Climate

The Mediterranean climate of Napa and Sonoma is characterized by warm, dry summers and mild, wet winters. During the summer months, temperatures can reach the 80s and 90s Fahrenheit (high 20s to mid-30s Celsius). It is essential to stay hydrated and wear sunscreen while exploring the vineyards and participating in outdoor activities.

Winter temperatures generally range from the mid-40s to mid-60s Fahrenheit (5 to 18 degrees Celsius). While rainfall is more common during this season, it is usually not excessive and contributes to the region's lush greenery.

Transportation Options

Getting to Napa and Sonoma is relatively easy, as they are located within a short distance from major cities in Northern

California. The closest major airport is San Francisco International Airport (SFO), approximately 60 miles (97 kilometers) from both Napa and Sonoma. Oakland International Airport (OAK) is also a viable option, located about 50 miles (80 kilometers) away.

Once you arrive, several transportation options are available to explore the region. Renting a car is a popular choice, especially if you want the flexibility to visit various wineries and attractions at your own pace. Many reputable car rental companies operate in the area, making it convenient for travelers.

For those who prefer not to drive, shuttle services and private tours are available, offering guided experiences to the best wineries and sights in Napa and Sonoma. Additionally, some hotels and resorts provide shuttle services for their guests, making it easier to navigate the region without a car.

Accommodation Recommendations

Napa and Sonoma offer a wide range of accommodation options to suit different tastes and budgets. From luxury resorts and charming boutique hotels to cozy bed and breakfasts and vacation rentals, you'll find the perfect place to stay.

In Napa Valley, the towns of Yountville, St. Helena, and Calistoga are well-known for their upscale accommodations and renowned dining options. Sonoma County boasts delightful lodging choices in places like Healdsburg, Sebastopol, and Sonoma, each offering its own unique charm.

It is advisable to book your accommodation well in advance, especially during peak seasons, to secure your preferred choice and avoid disappointment.

Safety Tips

While Napa and Sonoma are generally safe destinations, it's always wise to be mindful of your surroundings and take necessary precautions:

1. Stay hydrated, especially during the hot summer months, by carrying a water bottle with you.

2. Protect yourself from the sun with sunscreen, hats, and sunglasses.

3. If you plan to indulge in wine tasting, pace yourself and drink responsibly. Appoint a designated driver or use a guided tour service.

4. Keep your belongings secure and be cautious with valuables in crowded areas.

5. Follow the rules and guidelines of wineries and outdoor attractions to ensure a safe and enjoyable experience.

6. Familiarize yourself with local emergency contacts and medical facilities, just in case.

By being prepared and mindful, you can fully embrace the beauty and charm of Napa and Sonoma while keeping your travel experience safe and memorable.

CHAPTER 3

Napa and Sonoma are two of the most captivating and enchanting regions in California, known for their picturesque vineyards, world-class wineries, and breathtaking landscapes. In this chapter, we will delve into the top attractions that make Napa and Sonoma truly special destinations for travelers seeking a blend of luxury, relaxation, and cultural experiences.

Napa Valley Wineries

Napa Valley is synonymous with exceptional wines, and visiting its wineries is an absolute must for any wine enthusiast. The valley boasts over 400 wineries, each offering a unique and unforgettable tasting experience. From renowned estates to small boutique wineries, Napa Valley caters to every taste and preference.

One of the iconic wineries to explore is the Opus One Winery, founded as a joint venture between legendary winemakers Baron Philippe de Rothschild of Bordeaux's Château Mouton Rothschild and Robert Mondavi.

The winery is celebrated for its Bordeaux-style blends, and a guided tour here will take you through the art of winemaking and the estate's stunning architecture.

For those seeking a more intimate experience, the Castello di Amorosa is a medieval-inspired Tuscan castle surrounded by vineyards. This castle winery offers a captivating journey back in time, and a visit includes exploring the castle's underground cellars and tasting their exquisite Italian-style wines.

Sonoma County Wine Tasting

Sonoma County, just west of Napa Valley, is another paradise for wine lovers. With a more laid-back and rustic atmosphere, Sonoma offers a diverse range of wines, including Pinot Noir, Chardonnay, and Zinfandel. The region's wineries boast stunning views of rolling hills and vine-covered landscapes.

A must-visit winery in Sonoma is the Francis Ford Coppola Winery, owned by the famous director himself. The winery features an impressive collection of movie memorabilia, and visitors can enjoy a delightful wine tasting experience on the sundeck, overlooking the scenic Alexander Valley.

Another gem in Sonoma is the Ridge Vineyards at Monte Bello, renowned for its exceptional Cabernet Sauvignon and Chardonnay. The winery has a rich history dating back to the 19th century, and a visit here allows you to savor some of California's most iconic wines.

Historical Landmarks

Beyond the vineyards, Napa and Sonoma are steeped in history, with several historical landmarks that provide insights into the region's past.

In Napa Valley, the Old Faithful Geyser of California is a natural wonder that erupts regularly and captivates visitors with its mesmerizing display. Surrounding the geyser, you'll find charming gardens and a petting zoo, making it a family-friendly attraction.

Sonoma Plaza, in the heart of Sonoma town, is another significant historical site. It is the largest plaza in California and is surrounded by historical buildings, including the Mission San Francisco Solano, the last Spanish mission built in California. The plaza is perfect for leisurely strolls, shopping, and dining at local eateries.

Outdoor Activities

For outdoor enthusiasts, Napa and Sonoma offer an array of activities to explore the region's natural beauty.

In Napa Valley, a hot air balloon ride is an unforgettable experience, providing panoramic views of the vineyards and the valley at sunrise. Imagine floating peacefully over the picturesque landscapes, capturing breathtaking photos, and toasting with a glass of champagne upon landing.

For hiking enthusiasts, Bothe-Napa Valley State Park offers a network of trails through redwood groves and oak woodlands. The Ritchey Canyon Trail leads to a serene swimming hole, a perfect spot to cool off during warm summer days.

Sonoma County also offers a plethora of outdoor activities. Armstrong Redwoods State Natural Reserve is a must-visit, boasting ancient redwood trees and serene hiking trails. It's a place to reconnect with nature and find solace among these towering giants.

Art and Culture

Napa and Sonoma are not just about wine and nature; they also embrace a thriving arts and cultural scene.

In Napa, the di Rosa Center for Contemporary Art houses an impressive collection of modern and contemporary art. The center spans over 200 acres, with both indoor and outdoor exhibitions, featuring works by local artists and renowned names.

Sonoma also has a vibrant arts community, and the Sonoma Valley Museum of Art showcases works from local and international artists. The museum regularly hosts exhibitions, lectures, and art workshops, making it an engaging destination for art enthusiasts.

Additionally, both regions host various cultural events and festivals throughout the year, celebrating music, food, and the local community's talents.

Napa and Sonoma are an intoxicating blend of stunning landscapes, world-class wines, historical landmarks, outdoor adventures, and vibrant arts and culture. These top attractions make Napa and Sonoma truly exceptional destinations, captivating the hearts of travelers from around the world. Whether you're a wine connoisseur, history buff, nature lover, or art enthusiast, Napa and Sonoma offer an unforgettable and enriching experience that will leave you with cherished memories for a lifetime.

CHAPTER 4

EXPLORING NAPA AND SONOMA REGIONS

Napa Valley Highlights

Napa Valley, often referred to as the heart of California's wine country, is a picturesque region renowned for its vineyards, wineries, and breathtaking landscapes. Each town within the valley offers a distinct charm, and visitors are spoiled for choice when it comes to experiencing the region's rich cultural heritage and wine-making traditions.

1. Yountville

Yountville, a small but vibrant town in Napa Valley, exudes a luxurious and relaxed ambiance that makes it a favorite destination for food and wine enthusiasts. As you stroll down Washington Street, you'll encounter Michelin-starred restaurants and world-class tasting rooms showcasing some of the finest wines produced in the valley.

For an unforgettable culinary experience, make a reservation at The French Laundry, a three-star Michelin restaurant founded by Chef Thomas Keller. Indulge in a multi-course tasting menu that artfully combines local ingredients to create a gastronomic journey like no other. Additionally, Yountville boasts beautiful parks and art installations, offering a delightful blend of nature and culture.

2. St. Helena

St. Helena, with its charming Main Street, is another must-visit town in Napa Valley. This historic community features boutique shops, art galleries, and gourmet food establishments. Take a leisurely stroll along Main Street, exploring the unique boutiques and enjoying the inviting small-town atmosphere.

For wine enthusiasts, St. Helena is home to several iconic wineries, including Beringer Vineyards and Charles Krug Winery. Many of these wineries offer tours and tastings, providing insights into the winemaking process and a chance to sample award-winning wines.

Don't miss a visit to the Culinary Institute of America (CIA) at Greystone, where you can attend cooking classes, wine seminars, and dine at their restaurant that showcases the talents of the institute's aspiring chefs.

3. Calistoga

Calistoga, located at the northern end of Napa Valley, is renowned for its hot springs and spa resorts.

It's the perfect place to unwind and rejuvenate amidst beautiful vineyard-covered hills.

One of the most popular activities in Calistoga is to soak in the mineral-rich waters at one of the many hot springs and spas. Enjoy a mud bath or a relaxing massage for the ultimate pampering experience.

Apart from the therapeutic hot springs, Calistoga also offers excellent wineries and tasting rooms, providing a unique blend of relaxation and wine exploration. Castello di Amorosa, a medieval-inspired castle winery, is a standout attraction and offers a memorable wine tasting experience within its grandiose walls.

Sonoma County Gems

While Napa Valley gets much of the spotlight, Sonoma County, located just west of Napa, has its own distinctive charm and a diverse range of experiences to offer. Sonoma County is renowned for its laid-back vibe, stunning coastline, and thriving artisanal community.

1. Healdsburg

Healdsburg is a delightful town nestled in the northern part of Sonoma County.

Known for its picturesque plaza, Healdsburg offers a unique blend of wine, food, and art experiences.

The Plaza serves as the heart of Healdsburg, surrounded by boutique shops, art galleries, and gourmet restaurants. Spend time exploring the Plaza and the surrounding streets, where you'll discover an array of boutiques offering locally-made crafts, artisanal foods, and stylish clothing.

Wine enthusiasts will find plenty to enjoy in Healdsburg, as the town serves as a gateway to the Dry Creek Valley and Russian River Valley wine regions. Take a wine tasting tour, or simply wander through the vineyards and take in the scenic beauty of the countryside.

2. Sebastopol

Sebastopol, known for its bohemian spirit, is a charming town with a vibrant arts scene and a strong sense of community. Located in the western part of Sonoma County, Sebastopol offers a different perspective on the region's culture and lifestyle.

Spend a leisurely day exploring the town's art galleries and studios, where you can find unique works of art and crafts created by talented local artists. The town's liberal and eco-conscious atmosphere contributes to its alternative, yet welcoming vibe.

For nature lovers, the Laguna de Santa Rosa is a nearby wetland preserve that offers scenic walking trails and birdwatching opportunities. Experience the tranquility of the preserve and connect with nature in this peaceful sanctuary.

3. Sonoma

Sonoma, the town that shares its name with the county, boasts a rich history and is home to the northernmost Franciscan mission in California, Mission San Francisco Solano. This beautifully preserved mission provides a glimpse into the region's Spanish colonial past.

Stroll through Sonoma's Plaza, one of the largest in California, and explore its historic landmarks, including the Sonoma Barracks and the Toscano Hotel. The Plaza is a popular spot for picnics, live music, and community events.

Wine enthusiasts should not miss the opportunity to visit the Sonoma Plaza's tasting rooms, showcasing an array of local wines. The town's close proximity to a variety of vineyards and wineries makes it an excellent base for exploring Sonoma County's wine offerings.

Exploring Napa and Sonoma regions is a captivating journey filled with diverse experiences, from wine tastings at world-class wineries to immersing in the rich history and natural beauty of each town. Whether you choose to unwind in the therapeutic hot springs of Calistoga, embark on a culinary adventure in Yountville, or embrace the artistic spirit of

Sebastopol, both Napa Valley and Sonoma County will leave a lasting impression on your heart and palate. The next chapter will delve into the culinary delights of the regions, offering a mouthwatering exploration of the local cuisine and dining scene.

CHAPTER 5

CULINARY DELIGHTS

Napa and Sonoma are not only renowned for their picturesque landscapes and world-class wineries but also for their vibrant culinary scene. The region boasts a plethora of restaurants, eateries, and farm-to-table experiences that will tantalize your taste buds and leave you craving for more. In this chapter, we will explore the delectable culinary delights that await you in Napa and Sonoma.

Napa Valley Restaurants

Napa Valley is a paradise for food enthusiasts, offering a diverse array of dining options to suit all palates. From elegant Michelin-starred restaurants to charming cafes and bistros, there's something for everyone. One of the must-visit places in Napa is the legendary The French Laundry, a three-Michelin-starred restaurant that promises an unforgettable culinary journey. Reservations are highly sought after, so make sure to plan well in advance.

For those seeking a more casual yet delightful experience, visit Oxbow Public Market in downtown Napa.

Here, you'll find a bustling marketplace with numerous food vendors offering everything from artisanal cheeses and charcuterie to gourmet tacos and seafood. It's the perfect spot for a leisurely lunch or a quick bite between wine tastings.

Sonoma County Eateries

Sonoma County's dining scene is equally impressive, with an emphasis on farm-fresh ingredients and locally sourced produce. In the charming town of Healdsburg, you'll discover a wealth of culinary gems. Shed, a market and cafe, is a favorite among locals and visitors alike. Their seasonal menu celebrates the region's agricultural bounty, and you can savor everything from wood-fired pizzas to vibrant salads.

Another standout dining destination in Sonoma County is SingleThread Farms in Healdsburg. This exceptional three-Michelin-starred restaurant combines farm-to-table dining with luxurious accommodations for an extraordinary experience. With a focus on sustainability and Japanese-inspired cuisine, each dish is a work of art.

Local Cuisine and Specialties

While exploring Napa and Sonoma, be sure to indulge in the local cuisine and specialties that make this region unique.

Wine country cuisine often features dishes that complement the flavors of the local wines. Try dishes prepared with seasonal produce, artisan cheeses, and premium meats. The classic pairing of wine and cheese is an absolute must, and you can find numerous cheese shops and creameries that offer tastings and pairings.

Don't miss the opportunity to try dishes featuring fresh seafood from the nearby coast. Many restaurants in the area feature seafood caught that very day, making for an exceptionally fresh and flavorful meal.

Farm-to-Table Experiences

Both Napa and Sonoma take pride in their farm-to-table culture, where chefs and restaurants work closely with local farmers to source the freshest ingredients. Consider booking a farm-to-table dining experience, where you can dine right on the farm and enjoy a meal made from the produce grown on-site. These experiences often include tours of the farm, giving you a deeper understanding of the region's agricultural heritage.

In addition to farm-to-table dining, you can explore farmers' markets that pop up throughout Napa and Sonoma.

These markets are a feast for the senses, offering an abundance of fresh fruits, vegetables, artisanal products, and prepared foods. Strolling through a local farmers' market allows you to connect with the community and taste the true essence of the region.

As you indulge in the culinary delights of Napa and Sonoma, remember to pair your meals with the exceptional wines from the region. Wine and food are integral to the culture here, and the experience of savoring the two together is something to be savored.

The culinary scene in Napa and Sonoma is constantly evolving, with new restaurants and culinary experiences emerging regularly. Don't be afraid to explore and try new places, as you may stumble upon hidden gems that will make your trip even more memorable.

Whether you're a seasoned foodie or simply enjoy delicious meals, Napa and Sonoma's culinary delights will leave you with unforgettable flavors and memories that will linger long after your visit. So, prepare your taste buds for an extraordinary gastronomic journey through the heart of wine country. Bon appétit!

CHAPTER 6

Napa and Sonoma are synonymous with exquisite wine experiences, attracting wine enthusiasts from all over the world. Embark on a journey of the senses as you explore the picturesque vineyards, savor world-class wines, and learn about the art of winemaking. Chapter 6 will guide you through the must-visit wineries, provide tips for a seamless wine-tasting experience, and showcase the unique wine culture of these two regions.

Navigating Napa Valley Wineries

Napa Valley is a wine lover's paradise, boasting some of the most renowned wineries in the world. With over 400 wineries to choose from, planning your wine tour can be overwhelming. To make the most of your visit, consider the following tips:

a) Prioritize Your Preferences: Start by identifying your wine preferences. Napa Valley offers a diverse range of wines, including Cabernet Sauvignon, Chardonnay, Merlot, and Pinot Noir. Research wineries known for producing your favorite varietals to tailor your tour accordingly.

b) Make Reservations: Many wineries in Napa Valley require advance reservations, especially for tours and tastings. To avoid disappointment, book your appointments well in advance, particularly during peak tourist seasons.

c) Opt for Guided Tours: Guided tours provide a deeper insight into the winemaking process, vineyard management, and the region's history. Knowledgeable guides will enhance your experience and answer any questions you may have.

d) Explore Smaller Boutique Wineries: While iconic wineries are a must-visit, don't overlook smaller, family-owned boutique wineries. These hidden gems often offer personalized tours and a more intimate setting for tasting.

Sonoma County Wine Tours

Sonoma County is a captivating wine region, known for its laid-back atmosphere and diverse wine offerings. As you plan your wine tour in Sonoma, consider the following suggestions:

a) Discover Wine Trails: Sonoma County boasts several wine trails, each featuring a cluster of wineries with unique themes or varietals. Follow the trails to explore a variety of wineries in one area.

b) Attend Winery Events: Sonoma frequently hosts wine events, such as barrel tastings, release parties, and harvest celebrations. Check the event calendar for opportunities to mingle with winemakers and fellow wine enthusiasts.

c) Explore Sustainable Wineries: Sonoma County takes pride in sustainable and organic winemaking practices. Seek out wineries with certifications like "Certified Sustainable" or "Demeter Biodynamic" to support eco-friendly initiatives.

d) Picnic at Vineyards: Many wineries in Sonoma County offer picnic areas where you can enjoy your favorite wines paired with local cheeses and gourmet snacks. Take advantage of this delightful experience amid the vineyard scenery.

Wine Tasting Etiquette

Wine tasting is an art form, and following proper etiquette enhances the overall experience. Whether you're a novice or an experienced taster, consider these etiquette guidelines:

a) Pace Yourself: Take your time to savor each wine. Avoid rushing through tastings and allow yourself to appreciate the distinct characteristics of each varietal.

b) Use the Right Glassware: Wineries provide specific glassware for each wine type. Hold the glass by the stem to avoid warming the wine and interfering with its temperature.

c) Engage with the Tasting Room Staff: The tasting room staff are passionate about wine and are a valuable source of information. Don't hesitate to ask questions and seek their recommendations.

d) Avoid Wearing Strong Fragrances: Strong perfumes or colognes can interfere with the aromas of the wine and disrupt others' tasting experiences. Opt for a more subtle scent or go fragrance-free while visiting wineries.

Must-Try Wines of the Region

Napa and Sonoma are renowned for producing exceptional wines. To make the most of your wine-tasting journey, be sure to try these signature wines:

a) Napa Valley:

- Cabernet Sauvignon: Napa's crown jewel, known for its bold and rich flavors, often with notes of blackcurrant and oak.

- Chardonnay: Elegant and versatile, Napa's Chardonnay offers a balance of fruitiness and buttery characteristics.

b) Sonoma County:

- Pinot Noir: Sonoma County excels in producing high-quality Pinot Noir, characterized by its silky texture and red fruit flavors.

- Zinfandel: Known as California's heritage grape, Sonoma's Zinfandel showcases bold fruit flavors and a hint of spice.

Embrace the opportunity to sample these exceptional wines, and expand your palate as you discover the nuances and complexities that make Napa and Sonoma wines truly extraordinary.

CHAPTER 7

RECOMMENDED ITINERARY

Napa and Sonoma offer a plethora of experiences for every type of traveler. Whether you're a wine enthusiast, a foodie, a history buff, or an outdoor adventurer, this chapter provides a carefully crafted 5-day itinerary that will allow you to make the most of your visit to these stunning regions.

Day 1: Napa Valley Wine Tour

Kick start your journey with a full-day wine tour through the enchanting Napa Valley. Known worldwide for its exceptional wines, picturesque vineyards, and charming wineries, Napa Valley is a must-visit destination for wine lovers.

Morning

- Begin your day with a hearty breakfast at one of Napa's renowned cafes. Try the local favorite: eggs Benedict with avocado and a side of crispy bacon.

- Head to the first winery on your list. We recommend starting with a classic and iconic winery like Robert Mondavi Winery or Beringer Vineyards. Take a guided tour of the vineyard, learn about the winemaking process, and indulge in a wine tasting session.

Afternoon

- Enjoy a leisurely lunch at one of the many upscale restaurants or charming picnic spots amidst the vineyards. Savor delectable dishes paired with Napa's finest wines.

- Visit another vineyard on your list. Consider exploring a smaller, boutique winery like Frog's Leap or Chateau Montelena to experience a more intimate wine tasting.

Evening

- Relax and rejuvenate at one of Napa's luxury spas or take a scenic hot air balloon ride over the vineyards to catch a breathtaking sunset.

- Conclude your day with a delightful dinner at a top-rated restaurant featuring farm-to-table cuisine, perfectly complemented by a glass of local wine.

Day 2: Sonoma County Exploration

On day two, venture into Sonoma County, a charming region that boasts a diverse blend of vineyards, quaint towns, and natural beauty.

Morning

- Enjoy a leisurely breakfast in the heart of Sonoma, perhaps at the Sonoma Square, where you can savor mouthwatering pastries and fresh coffee.

- Begin your exploration by visiting the Sonoma Plaza, a historical gem surrounded by boutique shops, art galleries, and tasting rooms. Take a moment to visit the Sonoma Valley Visitors Bureau to gather information about the area.

Afternoon

- Embark on a scenic drive through Sonoma County's scenic countryside and stop at multiple wineries along the way. Consider visiting some family-owned vineyards like Benziger Family Winery or Chateau St. Jean for an intimate wine-tasting experience.

- Take a break from wine tasting and head to Cornerstone Sonoma, an innovative outdoor museum showcasing impressive landscape architecture and modern art installations.

Evening

- Relax with a wine and cheese pairing session at one of Sonoma's charming cheese shops.

- Dine at a restaurant renowned for its fresh, locally sourced ingredients, and pair your meal with a glass of Sonoma's finest wine.

Day 3: Relaxation and Spa Day

After two days of exploration and wine tasting, day three is all about relaxation and pampering yourself at some of the region's finest spas.

Morning

- Begin your day with a rejuvenating yoga session at one of the wellness retreats, surrounded by lush greenery and vineyard views.

- Treat yourself to a wholesome breakfast at a health-conscious cafe.

Afternoon

- Spend the afternoon at one of the renowned spas in the area. Choose from a variety of luxurious treatments, such as massages, facials, and mineral baths.

- Enjoy a healthy and delicious lunch at a spa restaurant.

Evening

- After your spa treatments, head to one of the local hot springs to unwind and soak in the therapeutic waters.

- For dinner, opt for a restaurant that specializes in organic and farm-to-table cuisine, ensuring a truly nourishing experience.

Day 4: Outdoor Adventures

On day four, immerse yourself in the natural beauty and adventurous offerings of Napa and Sonoma.

Morning

- Grab a quick breakfast or snack to go from a local bakery or cafe.

- Head to one of the nearby state parks or nature reserves for a morning hike. Jack London State Historic Park and Bothe-Napa Valley State Park are great options for nature enthusiasts.

Afternoon

- Indulge in a picnic lunch amidst nature's splendor or at a charming winery with a scenic view.

- Participate in an outdoor activity like horseback riding through the vineyards, kayaking along the Russian River, or cycling through the scenic countryside.

Evening

- Relax with a glass of wine and enjoy the sunset from a scenic viewpoint or a winery with a panoramic terrace.

- For dinner, opt for a restaurant with outdoor seating, allowing you to savor a delightful meal under the stars.

Day 5: Cultural Experience

On the final day of your journey, immerse yourself in the cultural richness of Napa and Sonoma, exploring the art, history, and traditions of the region.

Morning

- Start your day with a delightful breakfast at a cafe in one of the charming towns.

- Visit one of the region's art galleries or art studios, showcasing the works of talented local artists.

Afternoon

- Explore the historical landmarks of the area, such as the Sonoma Mission, Castello di Amorosa, or the Napa

Valley Opera House, to gain insights into the region's captivating past.

- Enjoy lunch at a restaurant known for its fusion of regional and international cuisine.

Evening

- End your trip with a memorable cultural event, such as a live performance at a local theater or a music festival if available during your visit.

- For your final dinner, savor the flavors of the region one last time, choosing a restaurant that offers both gourmet dishes and warm hospitality.

As your journey in Napa and Sonoma comes to an end, take with you cherished memories of exceptional wines, breathtaking landscapes, and the warmth of the region's hospitality. Remember that this itinerary is a mere guide; feel free to customize it according to your interests and preferences to make your visit truly unforgettable. Until next time, cheers to your memorable experiences in Napa and Sonoma!

CHAPTER 8

Welcome to Chapter 8 of the Napa and Sonoma Travel Guide! As you continue your journey through these picturesque wine regions, it's time to uncover some insider tips and local secrets that will enhance your overall experience and make your visit truly memorable. By immersing yourself in the local culture and following these hidden gems, you'll gain a deeper appreciation for the beauty and charm of Napa Valley and Sonoma County.

Hidden Gems

1. **Oat Hill Mine Trail**: If you're a hiking enthusiast, the Oat Hill Mine Trail in Calistoga is a must-visit. This historic trail winds through the hills and offers breathtaking views of the vineyards below. Remember to bring your camera to capture the stunning vistas.

2. **Jack London State Historic Park**: History and literature lovers will find solace in this hidden gem in Glen Ellen. The park is the former home of renowned author Jack London and is surrounded by beautiful gardens and vineyards. Take a stroll through the historic ruins and enjoy a picnic in the serene setting.

3. **Mystery Castle**: Tucked away in the heart of Sonoma, the Mystery Castle is an architectural wonder built from salvaged materials. The story behind its creation is as intriguing as the castle itself. Guided tours are available, giving you a glimpse into the eccentric life of its builder.

4. **Petrified Forest**: Journey to the Petrified Forest in Calistoga, where ancient redwood trees have turned into magnificent stone over thousands of years. Explore the trails and witness the fossilized remains of these majestic giants.

5. **Safari West**: Experience an African safari in Sonoma County! Safari West offers a unique opportunity to get up close and personal with exotic animals in a natural habitat. Take a guided tour through the savannah and encounter giraffes, rhinos, and more.

Budget-Friendly Options

1. **Free Wine Tastings**: Not all wine tastings come with a hefty price tag. Many wineries in Napa and Sonoma offer complimentary tastings, especially during certain times of the year or for specific varietals. Do some research and plan your visits accordingly.

2. **Picnic at Vineyards**: Instead of dining at expensive restaurants, pack a picnic and enjoy it amidst the beautiful vineyards. Most wineries have designated picnic areas, allowing you to savor local wines with a side of breathtaking scenery.

3. **Explore State Parks**: Napa and Sonoma boast numerous state parks with affordable entrance fees. Spend a day hiking, picnicking, or simply unwinding in nature's embrace.

4. **Local Farmers' Markets**: Discover the freshest produce and artisanal products at the local farmers' markets. Engage with the community, taste delicious treats, and maybe find some unique souvenirs to take back home.

5. **Cultural Events and Festivals**: Keep an eye out for cultural events and festivals happening during your visit. From art fairs to music concerts, these gatherings often offer free or reasonably priced entertainment.

Best Photography Spots

1. **Beringer Vineyards**: This historic winery in St. Helena is not only famous for its wines but also for its stunning Rhine House, an architectural gem.

2. Capture the beauty of the vineyards and the elegant building in your photographs.

3. **Lavender Fields**: During the blooming season, the lavender fields in Sonoma County create a dreamy, purple-hued landscape. These fields, such as Matanzas Creek Winery, make for incredibly photogenic scenes.

4. **Castello di Amorosa**: Transport yourself to medieval Europe at this enchanting castle winery. With its drawbridge, towers, and courtyards, this spot offers ample opportunities for capturing fairytale-like photos.

5. **Golden Gate Bridge Viewpoints**: While not directly in Napa or Sonoma, the nearby viewpoints of the iconic Golden Gate Bridge in San Francisco are worth the short drive. The bridge against the backdrop of the bay and city skyline creates an unforgettable image.

6. **Bale Grist Mill State Historic Park**: This historic mill in Napa Valley provides a rustic and picturesque setting for photography. The wooden waterwheel and vintage machinery offer a glimpse into the region's past.

Interacting with Locals

1. **Winery Tasting Room Hosts**: Strike up conversations with the friendly staff at winery tasting rooms. They often have fascinating stories to share about the winemaking process and the local culture.

2. **Farmers and Artisans**: Engage with local farmers and artisans at the markets. They are usually passionate about their craft and happy to discuss their products and techniques.

3. **Join Group Activities**: Participate in group activities like wine tours, cooking classes, or art workshops. These experiences create opportunities to meet fellow travelers and locals alike, fostering meaningful connections.

4. **Community Events**: Check out community gatherings and events, like town festivals or wine release parties. These occasions provide an authentic glimpse into the local way of life.

5. **Respect Local Customs**: Embrace the local customs and be respectful of the region's culture. Simple gestures like greeting people with a smile or using basic local phrases can go a long way in fostering positive interactions.

As you venture off the beaten path and embrace the hidden gems and local insights, your journey through Napa and Sonoma will undoubtedly become richer and more rewarding. Remember, the heart of any destination lies in its people and their stories. So, interact with the locals, savor the experiences, and create memories that will last a lifetime. Cheers to your extraordinary adventure!

CHAPTER 9

Napa and Sonoma are not just renowned for their exceptional wine and stunning landscapes; they also offer a delightful shopping experience. Exploring the local shops and boutiques can be an excellent way to discover unique souvenirs, handcrafted items, and artisan crafts that capture the essence of these charming regions. In this chapter, we will delve into the diverse shopping opportunities in Napa and Sonoma, guiding you to the best spots for finding that perfect keepsake to remember your visit.

Unique Souvenirs and Gifts

As you wander through the picturesque towns of Napa and Sonoma, you'll find an array of delightful souvenirs and gifts to take home with you. Whether you're looking for something to remind you of your wine-tasting experiences or a thoughtful present for loved ones, there's something for everyone.

1. Wine-related Souvenirs: It comes as no surprise that wine-related souvenirs are abundant in Napa and Sonoma. From beautifully crafted wine stoppers to personalized wine glasses, you'll find the perfect keepsake to remember your time in wine country. Look out for wine-themed art prints, coasters, and bottle openers, all of which make for wonderful gifts for wine enthusiasts.

2. Local Art and Crafts: Napa and Sonoma boast a vibrant arts and crafts scene. Local artists often sell their creations in small galleries or pop-up shops. Look out for hand-painted canvases, pottery, and sculptures that reflect the natural beauty and wine culture of the region. Purchasing locally-made artwork not only supports the artists but also allows you to bring home a unique piece of Napa and Sonoma.

3. Olive Oil and Culinary Treasures: Another culinary delight that Napa and Sonoma are known for is their high-quality olive oil. You can find a variety of olive oil products, such as infused oils, olive oil-based skincare products, and olive wood kitchen utensils. Additionally, keep an eye out for artisanal jams, honey, and other culinary treasures that make for excellent gifts.

4. Handcrafted Jewelry: Many local artisans specialize in crafting beautiful jewelry inspired by the natural surroundings. You'll discover pieces made from gemstones, metals, and even recycled materials that capture the essence of Napa and Sonoma's beauty.

Whether you're seeking a statement necklace or a delicate bracelet, the jewelry shops in these regions offer a wide range of options.

Artisan Crafts and Boutiques

If you have a penchant for artisan crafts and boutique shopping, Napa and Sonoma have you covered. These regions are home to a variety of charming boutiques and specialty stores that cater to different tastes and preferences.

1. Downtown Napa Shopping: Napa's downtown is a treasure trove of boutiques and specialty shops. Stroll along First Street and Main Street, where you'll find unique clothing boutiques, home decor stores, and gift shops offering a blend of contemporary and vintage items.

2. Sonoma Plaza Shops: The Sonoma Plaza is a historic gem with an array of boutique shops. You can explore stores selling handcrafted jewelry, artisanal chocolates, and gourmet foods. Don't miss the chance to peruse the bookstores, art galleries, and antique shops that add to the plaza's charm.

3. Healdsburg Shopping: Healdsburg is another haven for shopping enthusiasts.

Its tree-lined streets are dotted with boutiques featuring fashionable clothing, home goods, and local art. This is the perfect place to find trendy fashion pieces and unique home decor items.

4. Art Walks and Craft Fairs: Throughout the year, Napa and Sonoma host various art walks and craft fairs where local artists and craftsmen showcase their creations. These events provide an excellent opportunity to meet the creators and learn about their artistic processes. You can discover one-of-a-kind art pieces and support the local creative community.

Tips for Shopping in Napa and Sonoma

Here are some useful tips to make the most of your shopping experience in Napa and Sonoma:

1. Budget Wisely: It's easy to get carried away with the charming offerings in these regions. Set a budget for your shopping adventures to ensure you don't overspend.

2. Support Local Artists: Look for items that are locally made or sourced, as this supports the region's artisans and contributes to the local economy.

3. Check for Seasonal Sales: Keep an eye out for seasonal sales and discounts, especially during the off-peak months. You may find some excellent deals on unique items.

4. Ask for Recommendations: Don't hesitate to ask locals or your accommodation hosts for shopping recommendations. They often have valuable insights into the best places to find specific items.

5. Pack Smart: If you plan to purchase fragile or delicate items, bring some bubble wrap or packing materials to ensure they stay protected on your journey back home.

6. Enjoy the Experience: Shopping in Napa and Sonoma isn't just about buying souvenirs; it's also about soaking in the local culture and discovering the creativity that thrives in these regions. Enjoy the journey and the stories behind the items you encounter.

CHAPTER 10

Napa and Sonoma offer a wealth of travel resources to enhance your experience and ensure a smooth journey. From helpful websites and useful apps to tourist information centers and language tips, this chapter provides essential practical information to help you make the most of your visit.

Useful Websites and Apps

In the digital age, there are numerous websites and mobile applications that can greatly enhance your Napa and Sonoma travel experience. Here are some recommended ones:

1. Wine Tasting Apps: Explore apps like "Napa Winery Finder" and "Sonoma Winery Finder" to locate and learn about the region's wineries. These apps offer maps, ratings, and tasting notes, helping you plan your wine-tasting adventure efficiently.

2. Restaurant Guides: Discover the culinary delights of the area with apps like "Napa Valley Dining Guide" and "Sonoma County Eats." These apps offer comprehensive lists of restaurants, cafes, and eateries, along with reviews and menus to help you choose the perfect dining spot.

3. Local Events and Activities: Stay up-to-date on local events and activities with apps like "Napa Valley Events" and "Sonoma County Events." These apps provide information on festivals, concerts, farmers' markets, and more, ensuring you don't miss out on any exciting happenings during your trip.

4. Transportation Apps: Make your travel around Napa and Sonoma more convenient with transportation apps like "Napa Sonoma Vine" and "Sonoma County Transit." These apps offer schedules and routes for buses, shuttles, and other public transportation options.

5. Mapping Services: To navigate the region effectively, use mapping services like Google Maps or Apple Maps, which offer accurate directions and real-time traffic updates.

Tourist Information Centers

Throughout Napa and Sonoma, you'll find tourist information centers eager to assist you in making the most of your visit. These centers provide valuable resources, brochures, maps, and expert advice on attractions, events, and activities. Here are some notable tourist information centers:

1. Napa Valley Welcome Center: Located in Downtown Napa, this center offers a warm welcome and a wealth of information about the region.

Knowledgeable staff can help you plan your itinerary and answer any questions you may have.

2. Sonoma Valley Visitors Bureau: In the heart of Sonoma, this bureau provides detailed information about local wineries, restaurants, and accommodations. It's an excellent resource to start your Sonoma exploration.

3. Tourist Information Points at Wineries: Many wineries have their own tourist information points with friendly staff ready to share their passion for wine and the region. Don't hesitate to seek their advice on nearby attractions and activities.

4. Visitor Centers in Other Towns: Yountville, St. Helena, Calistoga, Healdsburg, Sebastopol, and Sonoma also have visitor centers that offer area-specific information, making it convenient to gather resources as you explore different parts of Napa and Sonoma.

Language and Communication Tips

While English is widely spoken in Napa and Sonoma, learning a few key phrases in the local language can enhance your travel experience and show respect for the local culture. Here are some language and communication tips:

1. Basic Greetings: Learn to say "hello" and "thank you" in Spanish, as you may encounter Spanish-speaking locals. "Hola" (hello) and "gracias" (thank you) are simple phrases that can go a long way.

2. Wine Terminology: Enhance your wine-tasting experience by familiarizing yourself with common wine terminology. Understand terms like "tannins," "varietal," and "appellation" to better appreciate the wines you taste.

3. Respectful Communication: Remember to be courteous and respectful when interacting with winery staff, restaurant servers, and locals. A friendly demeanor and a smile can create a positive impression.

4. Language Translation Apps: To bridge any language barriers, consider using translation apps like "Google Translate" or "iTranslate." These apps can help you communicate effectively, even if you don't speak the local language fluently.

5. Cultural Awareness: Take some time to learn about the local customs and traditions. For example, it's customary to tip at restaurants and tasting rooms, so familiarize yourself with appropriate tipping practices.

By utilizing these practical travel resources, you'll be well-equipped to explore Napa and Sonoma with confidence and ease. Whether you're discovering wineries, savoring delicious meals, or immersing yourself in the local culture, the information provided in this chapter will enrich your travel experience in this stunning wine country. Enjoy your journey!

CHAPTER 11

As you come to the end of this Napa and Sonoma Travel Guide, you may already feel the longing to experience the enchanting beauty and captivating allure of these two California wine regions. We hope this guide has inspired you to embark on a memorable journey through the picturesque landscapes, world-class wineries, and charming towns that make Napa Valley and Sonoma County truly exceptional destinations.

1. **Reflecting on Napa and Sonoma:** Throughout your travels in Napa and Sonoma, you will encounter a rich tapestry of experiences that will stay with you for a lifetime. From the moment you set foot in these renowned wine regions, you'll be greeted with warmth and hospitality, a reflection of the welcoming spirit of the locals. The diverse array of activities, from wine tasting and vineyard tours to exploring historical landmarks and indulging in culinary delights, ensures that every traveler can find something to cherish.

2. **A Feast for the Senses:** Napa Valley and Sonoma County are not just destinations for wine enthusiasts; they are a feast for all the senses. The breathtaking

vistas of rolling vineyards against the backdrop of the Mayacamas Mountains and the Sonoma Coast will leave you mesmerized. The fragrant aroma of the region's signature wines and the taste of fresh, locally-sourced cuisine will delight your taste buds. The sounds of laughter in bustling town squares and the touch of sunlight on your skin during leisurely outdoor activities will create unforgettable memories.

3. **The Heart of Wine Country:** Napa and Sonoma are undeniably the heart of California's wine country. The commitment to excellence in winemaking and the art of hospitality has turned this region into an internationally acclaimed destination. It's not just about sipping wine; it's about understanding the craftsmanship, history, and passion that go into each bottle produced here. The winemakers' dedication to their craft has elevated Napa Valley and Sonoma County to the pinnacle of the global wine industry.

4. **A Journey of Discovery:** Traveling through Napa and Sonoma is not merely a vacation; it's a journey of discovery. Along the way, you'll learn about the unique terroir that imparts distinct characteristics to each wine varietal, uncovering the secrets of viticulture and oenology. You'll gain an appreciation for the region's

rich history, from its indigenous roots to the Spanish and Mexican influences, and the subsequent evolution into a world-renowned wine region.

5. **The Warmth of Community:** As you explore Napa and Sonoma, you'll encounter a close-knit community that takes pride in its heritage and warmly embraces visitors. Local artisans, chefs, and winemakers are more than happy to share their stories and expertise, creating a genuine connection that transcends mere tourism. Participating in events and festivals, mingling with locals at farmers' markets, and engaging in conversations at family-owned wineries will immerse you in the genuine charm of the region.

6. **The Art of Itinerary Crafting:** While this guide provides a recommended 5-day itinerary, don't be afraid to let your own sense of adventure guide you. Create your own path through Napa and Sonoma, allowing spontaneity to lead you to hidden gems and unique experiences. Whether you're a wine connoisseur, an art enthusiast, a foodie, or an outdoor lover, you'll find abundant opportunities to tailor your journey to your passions.

7. **Memories to Cherish:** As you bid farewell to Napa and Sonoma, remember that the memories you've created will stay with you for a lifetime. The shared laughter, the stunning landscapes, the delectable wines, and the new friendships forged along the way will be cherished for years to come. Take a piece of Napa and Sonoma with you in your heart, and whenever you uncork a bottle from this region, let it transport you back to the magical moments you experienced here.

Napa Valley and Sonoma County are not just destinations; they are an experience that awakens the senses and touches the soul. Embrace the spirit of adventure, savor the flavors of the land, and immerse yourself in the warmth of the local community. Whether you come for the wine, the food, the scenery, or the camaraderie, Napa and Sonoma will leave an indelible mark on your heart. So, plan your journey, pack your bags, and get ready to embark on a remarkable voyage through the heart of California's wine country. Cheers to your unforgettable Napa and Sonoma adventure!

Printed in Great Britain
by Amazon

27407910R00036